Stephen Markwick and Fiona Beckett

A Very Honest Cook

Recipes and stories from 35 years at the stove

Foreword by Simon Hopkinson

culinaria press

To Judy
None of my 30 years in our three restaurants would have been possible without Judy,
so I dedicate these ramblings to her and thank her for letting me concentrate only on the cooking
whilst she has taken care of the rest of the business.

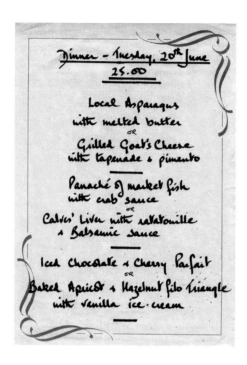

Markwicks Restaurant fixed price dinner menu, early 1990s

First published in Great Britain in 2009 by Culinaria press
1 Chandos Road, Redland, Bristol BS6 6PG

ISBN 978-0-9564089-0-7

Text copyright © Stephen Markwick and Fiona Beckett 2009

Photography copyright © Fiona Beckett 2009

Design and layout © Vanessa Courtier 2009

Stephen Markwick and Fiona Beckett assert their right to be identified as the authors of this Work in accordance with the
Copyright, Designs and Patents Act 1988

A CIP catalogue record for this book is available from the British Library

Printed and bound by Cromwell Press Group, Trowbridge, Wiltshire

Contents

A note about ingredients and measurements

As everyone will tell you it's difficult for chefs to write recipes because we're not used to measuring anything exactly (which is why Fiona, as an established cookery writer has been involved!) You should obviously feel free to adapt the ingredients and quantities to your own taste. Tasting as you go along is key to good cooking.

Some general information, not included in every recipe: When I say salt I mean seasalt and pepper should be freshly ground – I usually mix white and black peppercorns together. I generally use olive oil, a basic one (Spanish, Hojiblanca) for cooking, a better one for dressings (Greek, organic extra virgin, first cold pressed) both of which we sell in the shop. Cooking wine can be inexpensive but should be drinkable! I always use fresh herbs and whole spices wherever possible. Eggs are medium unless otherwise stated and cream always double! (No point in using it otherwise . . .)

How the book came about

As a food writer Stephen Markwick was always on my radar although I never managed to get to one of his restaurants until Culinaria. After my first visit four years or so ago, I was hooked by the intense, vibrant flavours of his cooking. Subsequent visits to Bristol revolved round getting a booking (by no means easy) and when we moved to Bristol I admit one of the attractions of the flat we had rented was that it was within half a dozen minutes walk of the restaurant. We became regulars.

I remember fabulously fresh-tasting salads (it always struck me as surprising that such a big man could conjure up something so delicate), wonderful, wobbly creamy quiches, unusual but addictive dishes such as cucumber fritters and sand eels, perfectly cooked, crisp-skinned pieces of fish, sauces rich with wine and spices and game, always game . . . There was even the odd pudding. (Stephen is not much of a man for puddings as his nearest and dearest will freely admit but he makes a summer pudding to die for.)

It struck me that it was sad that this wonderful food, which represents the best in the modern British cooking tradition, should go unrecorded. And not just the food: the whole Culinaria experience. Judy's welcome and the seamlessly efficient way she runs the place is an equal factor in making this very special restaurant what it is. I suggested to Stephen and Judy, by now good friends, that we should collaborate on a book and happily they agreed.

We also agreed about the type of book. Being the absurdly modest man that Stephen is, it seemed inappropriate to publish a large, glossy chef's book. We wanted a book that told his and Judy's story and enabled everyone who loves their restaurants to recreate their food. (In the unlikely event that they should wish to do so. While Stephen is there to make it for you why on earth would you bother?) We liked the idea that people could buy it for not much more than the price of a starter so we decided on a short book with the possibility of publishing subsequent volumes. To keep the cost down I've taken the photographs – a learning curve for me.

Pinning a chef down to precise measurements, of course, isn't easy. They cook intuitively, imperceptibly changing a dish every time they make it and Stephen is no exception. The recipes that were the original inspiration for these dishes – often Elizabeth David – assume a substantial body of cooking experience that many people simply don't have these days so we've erred on the side of spelling everything out at length to make sure that what you cook tastes as closely as possible to the way it does at Culinaria.

Above all this is a record of a career, an era, a very special cook – not a chef – and a partnership that has managed to make every customer feel cherished. I'm grateful to have experienced it.

Fiona Beckett October 2009

Foreword by Simon Hopkinson

" I first met Stephen and Judy Markwick with our mutual, late great friend, the wine merchant Bill Baker, of Reid Wines. I think Bill had suggested a proper, long lunch [is there any other?] at his Bristol restaurant 'Markwicks'. Although I had long been aware of Stephen and Judy as restaurateurs, with fine pedigree and culinary good taste from reading reviews of their previous establishment, Bistro Twenty One [also in Bristol, opening in 1980] in The Good Food Guide, I had no idea quite how revelatory my introduction to Stephen's cooking would turn out to be.

Stephen is one of the most honest cooks I know. And I say 'cook', because that, I think, is the description we might both prefer to that of 'chef'; the translation from the French is simply 'chief', anyway and, even though he has clearly always run a fine kitchen, a more benign description of Stephen is that he cooks. His manner is surely one of nurturing, encouragement and development of those around and with him, rather than a present day prima donna, of whom one can, quite soon, become heartily sick and tired.

His mentor, the late - and very great indeed - George Perry-Smith, who opened the Hole in the Wall in Bath in 1952, would later employ Stephen at his final restaurant [with rooms] The Riverside, in the fishing village of Helford, Cornwall, towards the end of the 1970's. Although Stephen had already spent time working with the marvellous Joyce Molyneux [who had also worked with GP-S at The Hole] at The Carved Angel in Dartmouth, and also running the kitchen at George Perry-Smith's leased café within The Bristol Guild, it was surely to be his two seasons spent in Cornwall with the master himself, that would leave the most indelible stamp.

Although I properly only ever met George Perry-Smith once, when he and his wife celebrated their marriage with a dinner afterwards at Bibendum, in 1990 [the honour will remain forever], his cooking and recipes had always had an enormous influence on me. I first ate lunch at The Hole in the Wall in 1971, aged 17, with a chum who had just finished his schooling at the nearby Prior Park College.

I ate smoked salmon tart, guinea fowl with apples, Calvados and cream and finished with Saint Emilion au chocolat – all as vivid now as it was then. His famous cold table was a feast to behold and I recall that the wine list was fixed to the outside of an empty claret magnum. The evening before, just to be on the safe side, I had called in to confirm my booking, I found the proprietor himself changing a light bulb in the upstairs sitting room. His bonhomie and charisma were evident in just a few words: "How very kind. Thank you so much. We shall look forward to welcoming you tomorrow." I, blushingly, was lost for words as I stumbled down the stairs...

Looking now at a copy of an enormous, pre-decimal menu [chicken roasted in tarragon butter, 16/6], it is plain to any intelligent and keen cook that here were a list of dishes that quite beggared belief in their breadth and range - as well as how the menu was worded:

"Meat and Birds - Usually", seven dishes [on the other side of the menu there are a further nine: "Sometimes"] then followed by this: "We think these dishes are adequately garnished, but you may like to add or follow with: [say] gratin dauphinois [correct spelling, naturally, unlike constantly misspelt, today]; brown lentils with parsley butter; aubergines; chicory; mushrooms; beetroot – and sometimes other vegetables." Oh that menus could read like this nearly 50 years later.

Well, maybe more diminutive and concise, but nevertheless sensitively displayed, Stephen and Judy Markwick present a menu that, without doubt, firmly has its roots in the stylish simplicity of George Perry-Smith's original: his fish soup, almost always; a slow braise of squid in red wine, orange and fennel [quietly superb]; deep-fried cucumber with dill and sour cream [astonishingly good]; goose à la Poitevine [very rich, an Elizabeth David recipe]; rissoles à la Parisienne [sweetbreads] with a glass of Marsala and a cup of consommé [uniquely GP-S] and, of course, salmon in pastry with currants and ginger, sauce messine - possibly the most classic and most loved of all. Stephen cooked dozens of these for Bill Baker and myself when we celebrated both our 40th and 50th birthdays. Leftovers kept each of us going for days...

Elizabeth David was, without doubt, an enormous influence on George Perry-Smith's menus - and also continues to so infect Stephen, myself and countless others. However, that which placed him in a class of his own was great élan, exceptional good taste and, last but not least, an innate sense of simple good housekeeping - a quality sadly lacking in many professional kitchens, today; his salmon and mushroom cutlet recipe bears testament to that.

George Perry-Smith's legacy continues to startle and inspire to this day. And Stephen Markwick, quite clearly, holds this precious inheritance close to his heart. 〞

Simon Hopkinson

35 years in the kitchen

Simon Hopkinson describes him as "one of the most honest cooks I know". The legendary Times restaurant critic Jonathan Meades called him "a superb chef" and regularly awarded him his highest ratings. So how come Stephen Markwick isn't a household name?

A big part of the reason must be that he's ridiculously self-effacing. Not for him the bright lights of the TV studio or the glad-handing tour of the dining room at the height of service. As Meades put it in a review of his former restaurant, Markwicks "he is temperamentally indisposed to tell the world how good he is".

If you're lucky you'll catch a glimpse of him at the end of the evening in his bespattered chef's whites, his shy smile an acknowledgement you liked his food. Which of course you did. It's what has made Culinaria, a tiny unprepossessing bistro in a side road of a residential area of Bristol a place of pilgrimage for some of the most respected names in the restaurant business.

It so easily might not have ended up that way. Stephen was destined for a career in accountancy, not food. Born in 1947 in London (Bedford Gardens, Kensington to be precise), his family moved to Alderley Edge where his father worked as a company director for the English Sewing Cotton Company.

He had a conventional upper middle class childhood of prep school and public school and would no doubt have followed in his father's footsteps but for the fact that his mother bought a hotel in the village called The Edge Hotel.

Young Markwick and his siblings (one brother, two sisters) were roped in to help - pot washing, peeling potatoes, laying tables and even cleaning cars. The business allowed his father to give free rein to his interest in wine (he even wrote a small booklet on the subject 'Guide to the wines of Burgundy and Bordeaux'), an interest he clearly passed on to his son. "We used to bottle our own house wine in the cellar" Stephen remembers.

Although he was always a good trencherman his interest in cooking was instigated by his grandmother, a formidable figure who brought up her three children single-handed after Stephen's grandfather died prematurely. Although she had 12 grandchildren, she and Stephen were particularly close and he used to visit her regularly in London. "I can remember sitting on the number 14 bus going to the Planetarium and coming home to have supper and play Cribbage" he says. She also inspired the frugal habits that have lasted a lifetime and a lasting love for offal. "She cooked cuts of meat that nobody else did at the time."

His teenage years saw him move between various boarding schools, first in Scotland (one that, subsequently closed down though not down to Stephen's antics, it appears) and then in Wales. By his own admission, he was sporty rather than academic, a keen rugby and cricket enthusiast who played for the first eleven. There seem to have been the usual schoolboy japes. "I remember climbing expeditions that ended up in the pub - the masters in one bar, the boys in another."

At 16 with one 'O' level ("Geography - the only one I thought I'd failed") there seemed little point in continuing his academic career so his father despatched him to work for the engineering firm Ferranti's, studying accountancy at night school. "It was hell. I hated every minute!" he says simply.

A face-saving exit was found in the form of a four year national diploma in hotelkeeping and management at the Ealing Hotel and Catering School at which he learnt all sides of the business including training as a chef. His first work placement was at the Savoy under the legendary Silvano Trompetto. "He was actually a very nice man" Stephen recalls. "He could speak to every chef in the kitchen in their own language – and there were 120 in the kitchen. I started as the seventh commis [chef] on the *poisson chaud* (hot fish section) chopping parsley, peeling shallots and turning potatoes. I loved it. if you got on with the *chef de partie* you were alright. I can remember Trompetto saying 'I've been watching you in the kitchen for a few days and you're always looking for jobs to do.' There was a coal-fired oven and it was my job to stoke the stove. By golly it could get the heat up when we needed to do a banquet!"

In another placement he worked at Claridges as a waiter. "That was a learning curve too. The kitchen was in the basement and there were really steep steps down to it. There was a way of holding your tray so you could go whizzing down to the bottom on the bannisters! I had one bad accident for which I thought I would be sacked. I was carrying a bowl of pasta and managed to drop it down a customer's back but amazingly they let me get away with it."

On leaving college he went to work as a management trainee with British Transport hotels, first in Aberdeen, then in Glasgow. It was at this point that he met Judy. "My mother had insisted that I came back for my sister's 21st and I didn't particularly want to go." he remembers. However, having spotted Judy, a friend of his sister who was working as a secretary in Brussels he was immediately smitten. "He kept phoning me up and proposed on New Year's Eve, the third time we met." Judy recalls "We were married six months later".

Their first home was in Stratford-on-Avon where Stephen worked at the Welcombe Hotel. At first Judy revelled in her new life. "When Stephen was on duty at the weekends I could join him and wallow in the luxury of room service!" Newcastle, their next move, was less appealing "bitterly cold and I didn't know a soul" and Stephen was rapidly becoming disillusioned with his career. "I was spending my life relieving hotel managers round the country and attending managers' meetings. The further you went up the management scale the more time you spent producing budgets and figures. I realised I was going to be really miserable if I carried on doing that for the rest of my life."

It was at this point that their lives changed for good. Stephen had spotted an advertisement in the Times for a chef to work for George Perry-Smith who had founded the Hole in the Wall at Bath, a restaurant he recalled having visited when his sister was at school nearby. "I remember reading the Good Food Guide and thinking I'd like to work there." He was offered a job at a new restaurant Perry-Smith was opening in Dartmouth with his protegée Joyce Molyneux - The Carved Angel. At first Stephen and Judy, who had just had their first child Claire, turned it down for financial reasons but serendipitously the letter never got through. Tom Jaine, Perry-Smith's stepson who was managing the restaurant, rang up and said "Are you coming or not?' They went.

> " He was always serious and keen - I don't think he's changed at all"
> Do you discuss food when you see him? "Oh, yes! Yes, of course. It's the
> most important thing in life. "
>
> Joyce Molyneux

How come they gave him the job? After all he had only a very limited experience of working as a chef. "Well I think he was the only one who applied" jokes Jaine. "Bright middle-class boys from London didn't come out to the sticks and no-one had heard of Joyce. We needed a nice chap who could cook. He was wonderful because he knew things about the great wide world of catering and he was prepared to do anything. In the '70s many chefs had never eaten in a restaurant which is why restaurant cooking was so bloody awful."

The next couple of years, Stephen and Judy both acknowledge were the most difficult of their lives: unbelievably tough for Judy who had given up work, just had their second child Zoë and was living on a shoestring, totally engrossing for Stephen. "Having done a 15 hour day he would go to bed with Elizabeth David and read her from cover to cover. He was excited by everything at the restaurant - the freshness, the smells, the colour of the food, seeing the fishermen coming in off the boats" says Judy. "He was totally and utterly engulfed - it was like being married to somebody else."

Professionally his relationship with Molyneux was a real meeting of minds. "Joyce herself is shy and self-deprecating and has never shown off about her talents" says Judy. "I think she could see a kindred spirit in Stephen." Molyneux bears that out. "He was serious and keen to learn - a pleasure to have around. From Stephen's point of view "there was always communication: Joyce was always talking about food, explaining what she was doing. Although George was very charismatic, it was Joyce who had the biggest influence on my cooking."

After two years at the Carved Angel, there were four more years with Perry-Smith, two at the café at The Guild in Bristol which Stephen describes as "quite revolutionary for the time, a bit like a Conran restaurant" then two years working alongside him at the Riverside at Helford. Again it was a seminal period. "Stephen had a wonderfully close relationship with George" says Judy. "He was a bit of a father figure: he took a real interest in him and Stephen, for his part, would do anything for George. He had a great aura, an incredible love and devotion to food as Simon has described so well."

Nevertheless, in 1979 the Markwicks decided, as many chefs do, to open their own restaurant. "We managed to scrape together the money to buy what is now Juniper restaurant in Cotham. Stephen's grandmother gave us £10,000 and the bank lent us another £20,000."

It was called Bistro Twenty One and was exactly the right restaurant at the right time. Both the customers and critics loved it. "It was the right price level and we were serving Elizabeth David-type food which was still new to the majority of people. It was packed all the time. (You can see the menus on the wall of their current restaurant, Culinaria. Many dishes on the menu there date from that time.)

It was at this point that Judy came on board as front of house. "Stephen wanted his own place and I realised that I would never see him if I wasn't part of it" she says. "By that time the girls were five and six so I was more free to be involved and we only opened in the evening. I used to put them to bed before I went to work and we had an au pair to look after them while we were at work. I still remember Stephen's mother sitting me down and making sure I knew what I was letting myself in for. She knew how it would affect our family life. And she was right - it did."

" Portions do tend to border on the excessive "

Good Food Guide 1983 in which they were nominated Bistro of the Year

"But I loved it and so did the customers. I remember one night we had the rain coming through the roof at the foot of the stairs and we rang them up to cancel their tables but they said 'We still want to come. We'll being our umbrellas'. It was extraordinary. When it was voted Bistro of the Year by the Good Food Guide it became the talk of London. We had people driving down to eat even though the petrol cost more than the food!"

So why did they sell it in 1987? "I don't know really" admits Stephen. "We shouldn't have done. We were full every night. We had 24 seats and were doing 30 covers a night, 40-50 at weekends. I suppose it had lost its excitement and become boring and predictable. We felt we needed more of a challenge,

Bistro Twenty One

Watercress soup	70
Provençale fish soup with aioli & sauce rouille	1.00
Chicken liver pâté	85
Spinach & cream cheese pancakes	85
Chicory with ham & cheese	85
Mushrooms Armenienne	85
Brandade of smoked mackerel	95

~

Brill with crab sauce	4.75
Noisette of pork 'Avesnoise', topped with cheese	4.25
Venison, pheasant & steak pie	4.50
Coq au vin	3.80
Best end of lamb, rare roasted with rosemary, served with ratatouille	9.00 (for 2)
Bœuf Bourgignon	4.25
Pheasant with port & celery	5.00
Goose 'à la Poitevine', with chestnuts & sugared almonds	6.00
Entrecôte steak with shallot & red wine sauce	5.00

~

All main courses served with either rice or potatoes, fresh vegetables or salad, as appropriate.

All prices inclusive of Value Added Tax

3/12/80

a better, bigger place where we could serve lunches, do food that was more ambitious and charge a bit more. Businessmen were starting to go out to lunch and we knew they wouldn't come to Bistro Twenty One for a smart business lunch."

They found the restaurant they were looking for right in the heart of the city in Corn Street where they went into partnership with fellow chef Andy Hunt - who Stephen had met while working at Harvey's where he was the head chef. It augured well: he was a Bristolian, had cooked at the top level they were aiming for and they got on really well but it turned out to be a disaster.

Both sides went their separate ways and Markwick & Hunt became Markwicks, very rapidly gaining the sort of accolades that Bistro Twenty One had attracted, particularly from the Times critic Jonathan Meades who awarded them 9/10 and made it his restaurant of the year in 1995. He wrote:

"There is a tradition of West Country Franco-English cooking which derives from the Hole in the Wall at Bath 20-40 years ago. Stephen Markwick is its most able current exponent which isn't to say that he's not his own man: he has raised this idiom to unprecedented heights. This is the most soothing, most relaxedly correct of restaurants and one of the most consistently pleasing."

"It was very glamorous" recalls Judy. "The interior was designed by the previous owner who had installed a black ebony bar that had been specially made in Paris and shipped over. The lights were made of Murano glass and shaped like grapes. The BBC once used it for filming The House of Eliott."

"We had a lot of film and theatre customers there and the odd politician. I remember Monica Lewinsky coming in after she had been speaking at the Oxford Union. I thought Stephen was joking when he told me she had booked – it did cause quite a stir. But, more important to us, Elizabeth David came twice. I remember her writing a note afterwards, which I still have, to say how much she had enjoyed it."

Inevitably there were difficulties too. Judy couldn't be as involved as she had been at Bistro Twenty One as the girls were by then teenagers and she needed to be at home more, but finding the right manager was always a headache. As, more unexpectedly, were the ecstatic reviews they had been receiving. "After the Jonathan Meades review when he gave it 9 we had a lot of people coming in with very high expectations and you sensed some of them wondering 'What on earth for?' given that we didn't have a Michelin star. Good reviews are a mixed blessing."

The crunch though was that the character of the town centre was changing. The banks and offices of Corn Street were being replaced by loud bars. Customers began to complain that they felt uncomfortable being down there at night and Judy herself admits that she got fed up with 'washing the vomit off the doorstep'. After a long wait to find the right buyer, they sold - a nail-biting process.

I just love cooking. I don't know anything else. It's what I've always done.

(In an interview with Tamasin Day-Lewis in Waitrose Food Illustrated) August 1999

"We thought the sale wasn't going to go through then the call finally came at 4 o'clock on a Friday afternoon just before Christmas 2002" recalls Judy. "We had to be out by the Monday. The hardest thing was that under the terms of the deal we couldn't tell our customers or staff we were going. It broke my heart."

They took a much needed sabbatical during which they travelled to New Zealand and spent six months in Ireland helping a friend open The Good Things Café. Another restaurant of their own seemed unlikely. "We were seriously thinking about doing a market garden after being cooped up in a basement for fifteen years" says Judy. "Stephen's father had been a great gardener."

Events dictated otherwise. One day Stephen was cycling down Chandos Road and discovered John Raines, the owner of the then Red Snapper restaurant, was about to sell. "We realized we would be better off doing something that we knew, rather than embarking on an entirely new enterprise, so we went for it. Our enthusiasm for running a neighbourhood restaurant came flooding back."

Culinaria opened in 2004, offering the same style of bistro food they were serving in their Bistro Twenty One days. "We wanted a modern bistro which was casual and personal, with a short menu where I could cook the dishes I really liked. We didn't want two sittings anymore – we'd done that." says Stephen.

The takeaway was an unexpected by-product. "The restaurant was a 60 seater and we only wanted 30 seats. Customers had always been asking if they could buy fish soup to take away, which gave us the idea of doing a complete takeaway menu. It is actually a lot of work but we do get a great deal of satisfaction from it and we can dovetail meals for the takeaway with the dishes we're putting on the restaurant menu."

The next step, of course, is the unthinkable one. Closing the restaurant, but more than that, finally shutting the door on their careers as restaurateurs. Stephen is now 62, an age when most chefs have long since hung up their whites or taken a consultancy role. Yet, what would they do if there wasn't Culinaria?

Neither of them can really contemplate that. Nor can we . . .

Lunch & Dinner

culinaria...

Thursday 22nd — Saturday 24th October 2009

Bread & Olives (with oil or butter) 2.25

Starters:

Provençal fish soup, aïoli & sauce rouille	7.75
Scallops, artichoke purée, grilled air-dried ham	8.50
Game terrine, fig chutney	8.25
Twice-baked goat's cheese soufflé, beetroot & walnut Salad (v)	6.75

Main Courses:

Grilled Sea-Bass, spinach, fennel, squash & salsa verde	17.50
Rare-roast wild Mallard, red cabbage & quince	17.50
Boeuf Bourguignon	16.50
Butternut squash & radicchio risotto (v)	13.00

Desserts:

Walnut & treacle tart, clotted cream	6.50
St. Emilion au chocolat	6.50
Pear jelly, lemon syllabub	6.25
Sticky toffee pudding, praline ice-cream	6.25
Local cheese	7.75

1 Chandos Road Redland Bristol BS6 6PG

Mussel and saffron soup

This is a recipe I adapted from a leek and saffron soup which I have always liked. It came from Shaun Hill who I think got it from Robert Carrier (such is the way that chefs work!). It's a great autumnal warmer as the weather starts to draw in - almost a meal in itself. We get some lovely mussels coming up from the River Exe at that time of year.

serves   6

ingredients
1 kg (2lb 4oz) mussels
5 tbsp olive oil
25g (1oz) butter
2 shallots
a few sprigs of thyme
1 large or 2 smaller onions, peeled and finely chopped
1 large or 2 smaller leeks, well washed, trimmed and sliced
2 sticks celery, sliced
a few sliced fennel stalks (save the bulbs for another dish),
3 cloves garlic, finely chopped
a good pinch of saffron
a few parsley stalks (save the leaves for garnish)
1 x 400g tin of tomatoes
350ml (12fl oz) white wine
the mussel liquor made up to 1 litre (1¾ pints) with fish stock (see p.59)
1 dsp tomato purée
salt, pepper and lemon juice to taste
double cream and chopped parsley to serve

method
Wash, scrub and de-beard the mussels, discarding any that are open. Heat one tablespoon of the oil and the butter in a large pan, add a couple of sprigs of thyme and cook the chopped shallots until soft. Add the mussels and half the white wine, put a lid on the pan and cook over a high heat until the mussels open (3-4 minutes). Empty the mussels into a colander, saving the liquor for the soup. Discard any mussels that haven't opened, take the meat out of the rest and set aside.

soup
Heat the remaining olive oil in a large pan, add the prepared vegetables and garlic, cover the pan and cook over a low heat for about 10 minutes. Add the saffron, a couple of sprigs of thyme, the parsley stalks, tomatoes, the rest of the white wine, the fish stock and the reserved mussel liquor. Bring to the boil, adjust the seasoning if necessary (the mussel liquor may already be quite salty) and simmer for about 40 minutes. Blend in a liquidiser and pass through a conical strainer or sieve. Return to the pan and check the seasoning, adding lemon juice to taste. Add the mussel meat and reheat the soup. Serve with a swirl of cream and some chopped parsley. (It's up to you whether you sieve the soup or not but I always pass smooth soups. It gets rid of any stringy bits of celery and gives you a silkier texture.)

Provençal fish soup

If there's one recipe we've been asked for more than any other it's our fish soup. People say it's the best they've ever tasted. Judy's father used to order it every single time he came to the restaurant - as do many other customers. I do a deal with one of our fish soup obsessives, Hinton Williams, a fellow rugby fanatic. I give him batches of fish stock and in exchange he videos the rugby for me on match days and drops round the tape first thing on Sunday morning so I can watch it on my day off.

What makes it so special? Well, the main thing is it doesn't contain any shellfish which means that all the people who love fish soup but can't eat shellfish can enjoy it too. It relies on a very good fish stock (p.59) but that takes time to prepare and some people just don't like the smell of fish stock cooking in their house.

Once you've got all the spices it's actually quite an economical recipe. I suspect it derived from the war years when you couldn't get a great variety of fish but it's obviously had a Provençal influence woven in too. Like most of my recipes I learnt it from Joyce Molyneux when we were at the Carved Angel but I've spiced it up a bit.

We can never make enough because it's so popular in both the restaurant and the takeaway. It's always a problem trying to get the right fish trimmings for the stock but I can never take it off the menu. If I did I'd get lynched!

serves	4-6 but I've included the normal quantities I use in brackets so you can make a bigger batch if you want

ingredients	1 onion (2-3)
	2 cloves garlic, chopped (4-5)
	1 stick celery (4)
	1/3 of a cucumber, peeled (3/4 of a cucumber)
	1 small bulb fennel (1 large one)
	1 tsp each freshly ground cumin, fennel, dill and coriander seeds (1 tbs)
	small pinch ground fenugreek (large pinch)
	1/2 dried chilli (1 birds eye chilli), finely chopped
	3 tbsp flavourful olive oil e.g. Spanish (6 tablespoons)
	1 x 200g tin chopped tomatoes (1 x 400g tin)
	225g (8oz) smoked haddock fillet, skinned and boned (375g/13oz)
	1/2 bottle very dry white wine (basic French or Italian white)
	1.5 litres (3 pints) fish stock (1 gallon) (see p.59)
	'fish bits' (see method)
	1 tbsp each chopped parsley, dill, coriander and basil (2 tbs each)
	1 small pinch saffron (1 large pinch), soaked for 5 minutes in a little warm white wine or water
	juice of 1 lemon (juice of 2 lemons)
	aioli (below)
	salt and freshly ground black pepper

to serve	rouille (below)
	croutons (below)
	grated parmesan cheese

method	Cut the vegetables into smallish dice, add the ground spices and season with salt and pepper. Heat the olive oil in a large pan and fry the vegetables until beginning to soften then add the smoked haddock and fry another couple of minutes. Add the chopped tinned tomatoes and white wine and simmer for about 10 minutes before adding the fish stock. Bring back up to simmering point then continue to cook on a low heat for another half an hour.
	Finally check the seasoning and stir in the chopped herbs, saffron and lemon juice (unless you're going to freeze it – see opposite). Take the soup off the heat and whisk in aioli (opposite) to taste (about a tablespoon per portion). Make sure you do this off the heat or the aioli will split. Just before serving you can add some bits and pieces of whole fish for extra texture. I use the offcuts of any fish we have on the menu but you could use a chopped up salmon fillet or a few prawns if you eat shellfish. Sprinkle with chopped parsley and serve with pots of rouille, garlic croutons and grated parmesan.

tips	If you make the soup ahead and freeze it don't add the herbs and lemon juice until you heat it up. You may also want to check the seasoning.

Don't let the stock or the soup boil.

You need to get the bones out of the smoked haddock fillet. Even if you buy it boned there are likely to be some there. Just run your fingers over the surface and you'll feel them. You can pull them out but you'll probably find it easier to use a pair of tweezers.

aioli

This goes into our fish soup and creates the creamy texture that everyone assumes is cream but you can also use it with salt cod and cooked or raw vegetables Provençal-style. You can make it in a food processor but, if you have a decent-sized mortar and pestle, it's just as easy and more satisfying to do by hand. I also think the texture and taste are far better. It is easy to 'over-process' aioli or mayonnaise in a blender which can cause it to separate when added to the soup. The crucial thing is to have all the ingredients at room temperature.

4 large cloves garlic, peeled and roughly chopped, 1 tsp flaked or coarse sea salt, 2 large fresh egg yolks, at room temperature, 150ml (5fl oz) fruity extra virgin olive oil e.g. Provençal or Spanish, 150ml (5fl oz) sunflower oil, freshly ground black pepper

Put the garlic in a mortar with the salt and pound until you have a smooth paste. Work in the egg yolk. Pour the two oils into a jug then gradually drip the oil, drop by drop into the egg and garlic mixture whisking continuously as you do so. Keep on adding oil very slowly until the mixture begins to stiffen then increase the speed you add the oil to a steady fine stream. Once all the oil has been incorporated add a litle warm water, half a teaspoon at a time to lighten and loosen the mixture. For fish soup I add a bit more water so that it amalgamates smoothly and doesn't break up into globules or curdle.

rouille

2 whole roasted peppers from a jar or a tin, 2 cloves garlic, a finely chopped fresh birds eye chilli or 1/2 tsp chilli flakes, 10-15ml (a scant tbsp) olive oil, 1/2 tsp salt

This is really easy. Put all the ingredients in a liquidiser goblet and blitz until smooth. Check seasoning, adding a little extra salt or ground chilli to taste if you think it needs it.

garlic croutons

A good way of using up old bread. Cut into medium-thick slices and shallow fry them in a mixture of olive oil and sunflower oil until crisp and golden. Remove from the pan and while they're still hot rub with a cut clove of garlic then cut them into cubes. Put them in a cool oven to finish crisping up or cool, store in an airtight tin and refresh in the oven or a dry pan just before using them.

Leek and cream tart

We've always had tarts on the menus of our restaurants but this is a particular favourite. You may spot it contains a fair amount of cream but that's what makes it taste so good - I'm afraid you can't do a slimline version. A general point about tarts - they're much better made deep than shallow: you seem to get more depth of flavour and texture.

serves

8 as a starter, 6 for a main course

ingredients

1 x 20cm (8 in) part-baked deep savoury tart case (see p.61)
2-3 leeks with their leaves still on (about 300g/10½oz once thinly sliced)
1 large onion, peeled and thinly sliced
50g (2oz) butter
2 tsp chopped thyme
2 tsp chopped parsley
4 medium egg yolks + 1 whole egg
50g (2oz) each Gruyere and Cheddar cheese
400ml (14fl oz) double cream
salt, pepper and nutmeg

you will need a deep flan tin or ring and baking sheet
(don't use pottery or china quiche dishes – they don't transmit the heat well)

method

Part-bake a pastry case following the method on p.61 and leave on a baking sheet. Trim and wash the leeks thoroughly to remove any grit and shred them finely. Heat the butter gently and cook the leeks and thinly sliced onions for a few minutes (not too long as you are trying to keep the leeks green). Add the thyme and parsley and season with salt, pepper and a little nutmeg. Leave to cool a little before adding half of each of the cheeses, the 4 yolks and the whole egg. Mix well with a wooden spoon and pour in the cream. Stir well and taste, adding a little extra seasoning if necessary.

Carefully pour the mixture into the tart case, sprinkle the remaining cheese on top, then bake in a hot oven (200°C/400°F/Gas 6) for about 20 minutes. Turn the heat down to 180°C/350°F/Gas 4) for another 10-15 minutes. If the tart is browning too much move it to the bottom of the oven. It doesn't matter if it is still slightly wobbly when you remove it because it will firm up in the residual heat while you're resting it.

Rest before attempting to trim the pastry above the rim of the flan tin (see p60). Remove the outside of the flan tin or ring and slice the tart with a serrated knife. Or, for extra crispy pastry, return the tart to the oven for a few minutes before slicing.

＊ Obviously you're left with a fair number of whites from this recipe. We use them to make meringues for the takeaway.

You may spot it contains a fair amount of cream but that's what makes it taste so good - I'm afraid you can't do a slimline version!

Mushrooms on toast

Wild mushrooms have such a fantastic flavour they need little done to them. We used to serve them in puff pastry tarts at Markwicks when we employed a pastry chef: now we've gone back to Bistro Twenty One days and simply serve them on toast. We get them from a variety of sources: my current sous-chef Matai has found some great places round Ashburton in Devon but won't say where they are until he goes back to New Zealand!

At the time of writing (August), I have just received the first Scottish ceps and girolles, so I used them in this recipe but later in the year there are other types, such as blewitts, chanterelles and trompettes. In the spring we have morels which are one of my favourites but these need a creamy sauce to bring out their flavour.

serves   2

ingredients   150g (5oz) wild mushrooms
                1 tbsp olive oil
                25g (1oz) butter
                1 clove garlic, chopped
                1 heaped tbsp chopped parsley
                salt, pepper and lemon juice to taste
                2 thick slices of sourdough bread
                flavoured or plain olive oil (see below)
                watercress, rocket or other salad leaves to serve
                truffle oil and parmesan (optional)

method   Clean the mushrooms with a pastry brush or unused paintbrush (you should never wash mushrooms) and trim the stalks with a sharp knife. If you're using a larger mushroom like a cep, cut it into slices and halve the larger girolles and trompettes. Heat a frying pan, add the oil, then the butter then tip in the mushrooms and cook for a couple of minutes, shaking the pan to flip them over. Add the chopped garlic and parsley and cook a minute or two more then season with salt and pepper and a squeeze of lemon juice.

Meanwhile toast your bread (a sourdough loaf is good for this). I do it on a griddle having brushed the bread on both sides with olive oil that we have infused with herbs, garlic and chilli*) but you can use plain olive oil and rub the toast with the garlic while it is still hot. Spoon the hot mushrooms on the toast and serve with a few lightly dressed salad leaves or some watercress or rocket. You can add a few drops of white truffle oil and some parmesan shavings for an extra luxurious touch but don't overdo the oil or it'll drown the taste of the mushrooms.

* For those of you who want to make flavoured olive oil this is how I do it. Take a head of garlic and slice in half horizontally. Use either the top or bottom half, a halved chilli, a couple of sprigs of thyme and rosemary and a piece of orange zest. Pour over your oil and warm it gently. Cool and keep in the fridge in a large jar or a plastic box for up to 4 days.

Game terrine

I'm not going to pretend this is the easiest thing to rustle up for a dinner party but if you feel in the mood to experiment it's very satisfying to make and an excellent piece of housekeeping.

I can never go into a restaurant with terrine on the menu and not try it to see how it compares with ours. We use whatever bits and pieces we have available from other game dishes: this recipe is based on pheasant or venison but you can use other types of game (see below). You just need to plan ahead as the cooking and resting needs to take place over 2-3 days. I told you - it's a real labour of love!

serves

This should make two small to medium-sized terrines, depending on the size of your dishes - enough for 16-20 portions. (I use a cast iron Le Creuset dish)

ingredients

1 pheasant including its liver and heart
225g (½lb) venison
450g (1lb) belly pork
110g (4oz) pork back fat
16 rashers smoked streaky bacon
55ml (2fl oz) white wine
25ml (1fl oz) dry madeira or brandy
1 tsp chopped thyme leaves
2 tbsp chopped parsley
25g (1oz) pistachio nuts
10 crushed juniper berries
1-2 tsp quatre epices
a few green peppercorns
salt
1-2 shallots
2 cloves garlic
bayleaves for decoration

method

Writing an exact recipe for a terrine is hard because it depends on what you have to hand or can get hold of but I can point you in the right direction! I tend to use different game, according to the time of year. A September terrine might be based on grouse and partridge, a November one on pheasant and venison and possibly hare in December or January. In the spring we make a lighter version with lamb's sweetbreads, chicken or guinea fowl. As we buy most of our game long legged (undrawn - see p.45) we are able to save up the hearts and livers which we incorporate into our terrines. We also keep venison and other game trimmings aside in a marinade to add extra flavour. Making terrines in the restaurant is simple good housekeeping, which is why they're harder to make at home. It's actually more useful to give you a set of general pointers rather than a recipe, which you can adapt to the ingredients and quantities listed above

1 Proportionately, you need an equal quantity of pork and pork fat to the amount of game, i.e. half and half. Of the pork, at least half should be pork fat as this helps to keep the terrine moist. I sometimes salt some of the pork in a brine tub for extra flavour and colour.

2 You should cut as much of the meat as you can by hand (at least half), only mincing the tougher cuts such as venison flank and game-bird legs which you should pass through the coarse blade. (I don't know what the results would be like with a food processor - you'd have to take care not to over-process the mixture.) I usually mince these with some of the hearts and livers and some garlic and shallot. (You can also layer the livers in the centre of the terrine along with some of the good quality breast meat, marinated and cut into strips. This helps vary the texture and gives a good marbled appearance to the finished terrine.)

3 Seasoning: This is the hard bit! But also the part worth experimenting with. I tend to use a mixture of quatre épices (to roughly the Jane Grigson formula of 7 parts white pepper to 1 each of cloves, nutmeg and ginger or cinnamon) which I grind to a powder in a coffee grinder. I also add crushed juniper berries, a few green peppercorns and some pistachio nuts. You also need some alcohol - either madeira, brandy or white wine and some fresh herbs, all of which need to be mixed into your basic meat mix. After you think you have got the seasoning right take a small amount out, form it into a meatball, fry it and taste it, then you have the chance to adjust the seasoning if necessary. (You need to be bold with a terrine!)

4 Assembly and cooking: This will usually involve lining a terrine dish with streaky bacon rashers. These should be batted out as thin as possible and left overlapping the terrine (see picture) so you can fold them over the terrine to cover the top. Then half fill the terrine with the mixture and add a layer of the livers and strips of marinated meat before the final layer of mixture. Fold over the bacon, lay a couple of bay leaves over the top and the terrine is ready for cooking. However I like to leave it in the fridge overnight to allow the flavours to develop. I cook it in a bain-marie (shallow dish or tin) of water in a moderate to cool oven, starting the cooking at 180°C/350°F/Gas 4 for the first hour then turning it down to 150°C/300°F/Gas 2 for up to another hour. The terrine is ready when it is almost floating in its own juices and just firm to the touch. It is important not to overcook it or to cook it in too hot an oven or it will dry out.

5 Weighting: The terrine should be taken out of the bain-marie and left to cool. Once it's cold I like to weigh it down with some weights overnight in the fridge until set which makes it easier to cut without the slices breaking up or crumbling. If you cover the terrine with a layer of pork fat it will keep for at least a week.

Butternut squash and radicchio risotto

Those of you who know me will know that vegetarian recipes are not top of my list but risottos are and this is a good autumnal recipe similar to ones we have enjoyed in Italy. The sweetness of the butternut squash, which is partly added as a purée to deepen the colour, is nicely balanced by the bitterness of the radicchio. Like most restaurants we make risotto ahead and stop it just before it's cooked (see method) so that it can be heated through at the last minute - a useful tip for a dinner party.

serves	6

ingredients	1 large butternut squash
	1 small, hot red chilli, chopped
	3 cloves garlic, sliced
	2 sprigs of thyme and a sprig of rosemary or sage
	3 tbsp olive oil
	1 red onion
	1 leek
	1 stick celery
	50g (2oz) butter
	350g (12oz) carnaroli or arborio rice
	1 small glass dry white wine
	1 litre (1¾ pints) hot chicken or vegetable stock
	2 tbsp mascarpone
	25-50g (1-2 oz) freshly grated parmesan plus parmesan shavings to garnish
	1 head of radicchio
	salt, pepper and lemon juice to taste
	a little chopped parsley

butternut squash Preheat the oven to 200°C/400°F/Gas 6. Peel the butternut squash with a vegetable peeler, cut in half lengthways and scoop out the seeds. Cut the top halves into 1.5 cm (¾-1 inch) cubes for the garnish then the bottom half into bigger pieces (these will be puréed with some of the stock and added to the risotto while you cook it). Put the pieces on separate trays and scatter with the chopped chilli, garlic, thyme and rosemary or sage. Season with salt and pepper and drizzle over a little oil. Roast the larger pieces of squash until soft (about 15 minutes) and the smaller ones for 10-12 minutes, until just done then liquidise the larger pieces with some of the stock.

risotto Clean, peel and chop the vegetables into fine dice. Heat the remaining oil in a large pan, add the butter, tip in the vegetables and cook gently until soft. Add the rice and a little salt and pepper, stir well to coat the grains with the oil and butter then turn up the heat a bit and cook for a minute or so more. Add the glass of wine which should sizzle as the liquid hits the pan then once it evaporates begin adding the hot stock little by little until each addition is absorbed, stirring all the time. This should take 10-15 minutes but halfway through this process add the puréed squash. Check and adjust the seasoning after you do this.

to finish

When the risotto is almost cooked, and there's still a bit of bite to it, you can stop it cooking by turning it out onto a baking tray, then finish it off when you want to serve it. You need to spread it out thinly to stop the cooking process.

Heat the risotto with a little more stock, and add the mascarpone and grated parmesan to taste. Trim and shred the radicchio and add it at this stage (it will cook out in the heating up process) along with the remaining butternut squash cubes. (Alternatively you can reheat the squash cubes in a little stock and scatter them over the risotto when you serve it.) Check the seasoning again, adding extra salt and pepper to taste and maybe a little lemon juice. Serve in warm bowls topped with a few parmesan shavings and a little chopped parsley.

Culinaria fish pie

A fish pie is a good way for a restaurant to use up fish trimmings but having said that we're quite particular about what we put in it. We generally use pollock rather than cod these days unless Steve, our supplier, says it's been line-caught and I usually put in a bit of salmon and smoked haddock for flavour. Sometimes we add a bit of shellfish and make it with a crab sauce but basically it's a frugal recipe. It's one of the deli staples and my mother's favourite dish. Whenever we go to see her we take supplies to fill up her freezer!

serves 6

ingredients

225g (8oz) salmon
225g (8oz) pollock
2 shallots, peeled and chopped
white wine (optional)
225g (8oz) smoked haddock
570ml (1 pint) milk
1 bayleaf
a pinch of cayenne pepper
75g (3oz) spinach leaves
3 eggs
40g (1 1/2 oz) butter
40g (1 1/2 oz) plain flour
a squeeze of lemon juice
2 tbsp chopped fresh dill or parsley
50g (2oz) small North Atlantic prawns
salt and pepper
for the mash
700g (1lb 8oz) Maris Piper or other good boiling potatoes, peeled and cut into even-sized pieces
50g (2oz) butter
50-75ml (2-3 fl oz) milk
freshly grated nutmeg to taste

method

Heat the oven to 200°C/400°F/Gas 6. Put the salmon and pollock in a baking dish with the chopped shallots, salt and pepper and a splash of white wine if you have some to hand. Cover with a butter paper and cook for 4-5 minutes until just cooked*. Set the fish on one side and save the pan juices. Meanwhile cover the smoked haddock with the milk, add a bay leaf and a pinch of cayenne pepper, bring up to the boil and take off the heat. Remove the haddock from the milk and save the milk.

Wash and cook the spinach (possibly with a little leek or onion, if you have some) and drain thoroughly, squeezing out any excess moisture. Cover the eggs with cold water, bring to the boil and boil for 6 minutes. (If they're fridge-cold add a splash of vinegar to stop them cracking). Cool, peel and chop the eggs. Put the potatoes on to boil for the mash.

Next make a sauce using the milk from the haddock and any juices from the salmon and pollock. Warm the butter in a small saucepan, stir in the flour, cook for a few seconds then add the milk you cooked the haddock in bit by bit, beating well with a wooden spoon between each addition. Add any juices from the salmon and pollock and simmer for a few minutes then season with salt and pepper and a squeeze of lemon juice. Stir in the chopped dill or parsley. Make the mash following the suggested method below. Season well.

to assemble

To put the pie together break up the fish into large chunks, removing the skin and any bones. Put in a bowl with the spinach, eggs and prawns and pour over the sauce. Mix, taking care not to break up the fish too much, check the seasoning and turn into a buttered pie dish or individual dishes. We pipe the mash on to the top but you can equally well spread it over, roughing it up with a fork. Bake in a hot oven (200°C/400°F/ Gas 6) for approx 20-25 minutes.

٭ The key thing when making a fish pie is not to overcook the fish on first cooking. I like to bake it in the oven as it helps to keep its shape and you also get some good juices to add to the sauce. Pouring the sauce onto the fish rather than adding the fish to the sauce also helps as it doesn't carry on cooking and you can use just the amount of sauce you need.

how to make good mash

To make good mash you need Maris Piper or another good boiling potato. Peel and cut them into even-sized pieces, cover them with cold water and add a pinch of salt then bring them to the boil and simmer gently until just cooked. Strain them in a colander then cover with a lid and stand the colander over the pan on the stove to dry out for a few minutes. Pass the potatoes through a mouli-legumes or a potato ricer and return them to the pan. In another small pan heat 50g butter and 50-75ml of milk and beat into the potato. Season with salt, pepper and some freshly grated nutmeg. (If you don't have a mouli you can obviously use an ordinary potato masher or fork.)

Brill baked in cider with thyme, tomato and mustard

This recipe originally came from Colin White, a fellow George Perry-Smith disciple and friend of Jane Grigson's. I worked at his restaurant White's in Cricklade for a while after we sold Bistro Twenty One. He just rang out of the blue and said 'I've never met you or been to your restaurant but I wondered if you could come and help me out?' When I walked into his kitchen it was just like walking into my own. He used to come and help me at Markwicks in December when we got frantic. The mushroom caviar we make comes from him as well.

serves

4

ingredients

4 x 150g (5oz) skinned fillets of brill cut to the same thickness
2 tomatoes, peeled*
1-2 shallots, finely chopped
1 tbsp thyme leaves, finely chopped
4 tsp Dijon mustard
parsley breadcrumbs (see below)
25g (1oz) butter
150ml (5fl oz) dry cider (we use Day's cider from Bristol farmers' market)
a splash of fish stock (see p.59)
salt and freshly ground white and black pepper

method

Preheat the oven to 200°C/400°F/Gas 6. Put the brill fillets into a cast iron dish or ovenproof frying pan with what would have been the skin side upwards along with the chopped shallot and thyme. Season with salt and pepper. Spread a thin layer (about a teaspoon) of mustard over each brill fillet, then thinly slice the tomato and put 2-3 slices on each piece of fish. Sprinkle the parsley breadcrumbs over the tomatoes and top with a knob of butter.

Pour in the cider and a splash of fish stock if you have some. Bring to the boil then transfer to the pre-heated oven for about 5 minutes.

Once the fish is cooked remove it from the pan and keep it warm whilst you reduce the cooking liquor by approximately half. Add a couple of tablespoons of parsley and the remaining butter, shaking the pan or whisking as you do so. (This gives a richer finish to the sauce). I like to serve the fillets on a bed of spinach and some new potatoes.

* To skin tomatoes make a little nick in the skin of each tomato with a sharp knife, put them in a bowl and cover with boiling water. Count to 20 then drain off the water and cover with cold water. The skins should slip off easily

Squid with red wine, orange and fennel

A really popular dish both in the restaurant and takeaway. I think it's Catalan by origin but this version comes via George Perry-Smith. I make it slightly spicier than he did – the fennel and dill are my additions but then I'm always trying to boost the flavour of any dish I take on. You don't want to hold back on the salt either – squid can absorb a fair amount. If you leave it out – or add it at the last minute – the dish will taste bland or too salty.

I also suggest you buy your squid cleaned – it's a bit of a pain preparing it yourself. You can only cook squid very fast or slowly like this. Anything in between will be tough - like eating rubber bands!

serves

4 as a main course or 6-8 as a starter

ingredients

500g (1lb 2oz) prepared and cleaned squid
1 large or 2 smaller onions
4 cloves garlic
1 leek
½ bulb fennel
3 tbsp good tasty olive oil (I use Spanish for cooking)
1 dsp each fennel seeds, dill seeds and coriander seeds
  (or 1 tsp of each if ready-ground. If you can't find dill seeds use a little more fennel)
2 small hot bird's eye chillies, de-seeded and sliced or 1 tsp dried chilli flakes
1 tbsp tomato paste (plus a couple of tinned or skinned, fresh tomatoes if you have some)
2 oranges, zest and juice
½ bottle full-bodied red wine (nothing fancy but drinkable)
a small handful of fresh coriander
salt and freshly ground black pepper
for the orange gremolata
2 cloves garlic
a small handful of flat-leaf or curly parsley
grated rind of 1 orange

method

Pre-heat the oven to 150°C/300°F/Gas 2. Re-wash the squid making sure there's no grit left in it. Cut the body into rings, the wings into strips and leave the tentacles in longish pieces. Leave in a colander to drain.

Slice the vegetables thinly and fry in a casserole with the olive oil until starting to soften. Grind the fennel, dill and coriander seeds (if using seeds) in a pestle and mortar or coffee grinder and add the ground spices to the vegetables with the chopped chilli. Fry a couple of minutes then add the squid. (You need to make sure the vegetables and spices are hot before you fry the squid or it will stew rather than fry.)

Cook all the ingredients together briefly before adding the tomato paste, zest and juice of the oranges and red wine. Season well with salt and pepper (the squid will absorb a fair bit of salt). Bring up to simmering point then cover and cook in the oven for 1-1 1/2 hours until tender (the cooking time will depend on the size of the squid). Adjust the seasoning, chop the fresh coriander and add to the dish. Serve with either rice or croutons and a sprinkling of orange gremolata*.

* To make the gremolata finely chop the garlic and parsley and chop together with the grated orange rind.

In the restaurant we serve this with a tomato garnish as well as the gremolata. If you want to do this gently fry a couple of sliced shallots, add 3-4 peeled, halved or diced tomatoes and a splash of white wine, season with salt and pepper and fry until the wine has evaporated and the tomatoes are starting to caramelise. We put this on top of the squid and then sprinkle the gremolata on top of the tomatoes.

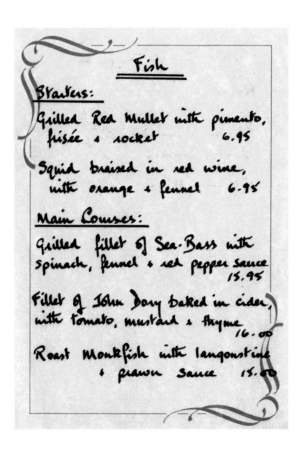

A daily fish list from Markwicks in the 1990s

Oxtail with grapes

An Elizabeth David recipe and a personal favourite that turns out a totally different way from what you might imagine from the ingredients. (The grapes create all the liquid so there's no need for wine or stock). The original recipe, which originated from the wine harvest, recommends soaking the oxtail for a couple of hours but I've never found the need to do that (oxen are probably younger these days). What you do need is a mouli-legumes – the consistency of the sauce won't be the same without it or if you try to use a food processor. They're not expensive though and useful for making other things like chicken liver paté and mash (see p.30)

Older recipes recommend soaking oxtail for a couple of hours but I've never found the need to do that. Oxen are probably younger these days!

serves	6-8

ingredients	225g (8oz) smoked streaky bacon in a piece or cubed pancetta
	4 onions, peeled and sliced
	8 carrots, peeled and sliced
	4-6 cloves garlic, peeled and finely chopped
	a couple of springs of thyme, 3 or 4 parsley stalks and a couple of bayleaves
	2 oxtail, jointed
	900g (2lb) white or black grapes
	$\frac{1}{2}$ tsp ground mace
	sea salt and ground black and white pepper

method

Cut the bacon into dice. Heat the oil in a large casserole and cook the bacon until the fat starts to run. Add the sliced onions, carrots, garlic, thyme, bay leaves and parsley stalks and fry together thoroughly. Trim the excess fat off the oxtail pieces, season, add to the pan and fry with the vegetables.

Take the grapes, keeping a few for garnish and crush them roughly by hand over the oxtail. Add a large pinch of mace and season with salt and pepper and stir. Check the seasoning, adding more if necessary. Cover the surface with a sheet of greaseproof paper then put a lid on the casserole and cook in a very low oven (140°C/275°F/Gas 1) for about 3-4 hours, until tender. (You want to get to the stage where the oxtail hasn't yet fallen off the bone but is about to.)

Remove the oxtail carefully with a slotted spoon and set aside. Remove the meat off any thin end bits of tail that could go through the mouli and mouli the sauce, passing it first through the coarse blade and then through the finer one if necessary if there are still any pips. Carefully spoon off any fat*, check the seasoning and pour back over the oxtail. Serve with some fresh, halved grapes (with the pips removed) and with mashed or boiled potatoes.

* Like most casseroles this improves from being kept for 24 hours so you could refrigerate the dish and skim off the fat the next day.

Beef bourguignon

Another George Perry-Smith classic I seem to have been cooking all my life – it's a very satisfying dish to make. The key – as with the fish soup – is a good stock (see p.58) and marinading the meat overnight. The herbs are important for flavour too. I sometimes add a bit more thyme, if I feel in the mood. Even if you're making this dish for two it's worth making this larger amount as it freezes well. Ideally serve it the day after you make it.

serves   10

ingredients

2kg (4lb 8oz) chuck steak or other braising beef
1 bottle of medium to full-bodied red wine
4 onions, peeled and sliced
6 cloves garlic, sliced
a handful of parsley with stalks
a few sprigs of thyme
1 bay leaf
3 tbsp duck fat or beef dripping
225g (8oz) piece smoked streaky bacon, diced or cubed pancetta
2 tbsp seasoned flour
2 level tbsp tomato purée
275ml (10fl oz) home-made beef or chicken stock (see p.58)
a splash of red wine vinegar
pork skin (optional)
bouquet garni
sautéed button onions and mushrooms (see below)
salt and pepper

method

Trim most of the fat off the meat and cut into large cubes. Place the meat in a bowl or shallow dish with half the wine, the sliced onions and garlic, a few parsley stalks, a couple of sprigs of thyme and a bayleaf and mix well. Leave overnight then drain the meat and vegetables in a colander, saving the marinade.

Separate out the pieces of beef ready for coating with seasoned flour. Heat a deep casserole or sauté pan. Add 1 tablespoon of the duck fat or beef dripping and the diced streaky bacon and cook over a low heat until the bacon fat starts to run. Add the marinated onions and garlic to the casserole and cook over a moderate heat for about 5 minutes until they start to soften.

Meanwhile toss the meat cubes in seasoned flour brown well on all sides in a frying pan in a little more duck fat or dripping, then add to the onions and bacon. Sprinkle over a little extra flour, and stir in the tomato purée. Put the marinade and stock in the pan in which you browned the meat, plus an extra glass of red wine, work it round the sides to deglaze the pan and strain it over the meat.

Bring to the boil and taste, adding a touch more salt and a splash of red wine vinegar if you think it needs it. If you have a piece of pork skin (without any fat), add that too – it gives the sauce a glossy sheen.

Cover with a lid and cook in a slow oven (140°C/275°F/Gas 1) for 2-2½ hours. Towards the end of the cooking time check the meat every 15 minutes or so for tenderness. If you have time, cool and leave overnight for the flavours to develop. Transfer to a clean casserole and add a splash of water before reheating it with the sautéed onions and mushrooms (see below).

We usually serve this with mash (see p.30) and braised red cabbage or cavolo nero.

sautéed onions Fry a couple of dozen peeled whole button onions over a low heat in a little butter and sunflower oil for about 10 minutes. When nicely browned add a good splash of red wine vinegar, a splash of red wine and season with salt and pepper. Cover with a lid and cook until tender. I like to add these to the beef just before I reheat and serve it so they don't break down and lose their shape but you can add them earlier if you prefer so that the flavours amalgamate better.

sautéed mushrooms You can just sauté the mushrooms in a little oil and butter – again you need about 24 for this quantity – but we usually cook them with some finely diced bacon or pancetta, finely chopped garlic, a little chopped parsley and a splash of red wine. Add to the beef, as above.

" I used to love the beef bourguignon so much (and still do) that I once asked Stephen if I could watch him make it. An unbelievable amount of time and care went into it. I remember being struck by his liberal use of herbs and spices and the fact he fried everything in duck fat but the key secret is that he covers the top of the pot with a layer of pig's skin which gives the dish a fantastic glossy sheen. "

Regular customer Simond ffiske

Spiced lamb with aubergines, chickpeas and apricots

This started life as an Elizabeth David recipe but has become more of a tagine over the years. I like the addition of turmeric and cardamom and the apricots give it a nice fruity note. You could leave out the chickpeas but they make it stretch further. A very popular dish in the deli and one which is well suited to making ahead as it reheats well.

serves   6

ingredients   110g (4oz) dried chickpeas, soaked or 2 tins of chickpeas, drained and rinsed
1 kg (2lb 4oz) boned lamb shoulder
1 tbsp each coriander seeds, cumin seeds and cardamom pods
   ground roughly in a coffee or spice grinder or with a pestle and mortar
2 good sized aubergines
2 onions, peeled and sliced
6 cloves garlic, peeled and sliced
3-4 tbsp each sunflower and olive oil
75g (3oz – about 12) dried apricots*
a pinch of saffron
250ml (9fl oz) white wine
1 tsp turmeric
1 tbsp tomato puree
1 x 400g tin whole or chopped tomatoes
400ml (14fl oz) lamb or chicken stock (see p.58)
2-3 tbsp each chopped mint and fresh coriander
a good squeeze of lemon juice
salt and pepper to taste

method   If using dried chickpeas soak them overnight then bring them to the boil in fresh water, skim and cook for about 1-1 1/4 hours until just tender. Cut up the lamb, trim off any excess fat and season it with the whole ground spices and salt and pepper. Cut the aubergine into fairly large cubes and sprinkle with salt. Tip the cubes into a colander under a weighted plate and set aside for 20-30 minutes. Rinse the aubergine cubes and pat dry.

Heat 3 tablespoons of the oil in a casserole, add the sliced onions and garlic and turmeric and cook over a moderate heat until soft. In a separate frying pan brown the meat in another couple of tablespoons of oil. Once the meat is browned add it to the casserole then tip the aubergines in the frying pan, add a little more oil and fry until they too have taken on some colour. Return the aubergines to the colander to drain off any excess oil and set aside to add later.

Cover the apricots and saffron with 100ml (3 1/2 fl oz) of the white wine or with water, heat gently and keep on one side.

Add the tomato purée and chopped tomatoes to meat and onions. Deglaze the frying pan with the remaining white wine and stock. Add to the casserole and bring it all to simmering point. Check the seasoning, then put a lid on the pan and cook in a slow oven (150°C/300°/Gas 2) for approx 60 minutes or until the lamb is just done. Add the cubed aubergine, soaked apricots, chickpeas, herbs and lemon juice and check the seasoning again. Either return to the oven for a another 10 minutes or leave on a very low heat to let the flavours mingle.

＊ Unsulphured apricots have a better flavour but sulphured ones have a brighter colour. It's up to you which you use.

to serve   We serve this with couscous or rice, sometimes flavoured with a little saffron, and some Greek yoghurt mixed with garlic and mint.

I like the addition of turmeric and cardamom and the apricots give it a nice fruity note.

Loin of venison with celeriac and potato mash and honeyed parsnips

Venison has featured regularly on our menu over the years and we have been fortunate enough to have the same supplier for the 30 years we have been in Bristol. He sources his venison from the surrounding countryside, in particular the Mendips. We prefer to use roe deer which are available throughout the year. They are always wild and never farmed like fallow or red deer can be because they're so small but that's an advantage as they do not need much cooking and don't dry out as venison can do. Hanging for a good week, sometimes up to two, enhances the flavour considerably.

In this recipe I have used the loin because it is flavoursome and very easy to prepare and cook. In the restaurant I combine it with some of the leg so the customer has a little of each. The rest of the leg goes in terrines, sausages and pies. (That's the beauty of having a commercial kitchen as one is able to use up all the parts of the animal!)

I often put it on the menu in the run-up to Christmas as my concession to a Christmas menu and add a few cranberries . . .

serves   6

ingredients

1 saddle of roe deer (or a loin of venison if it comes from a larger deer)

for the marinade

3 tbsp olive oil

2 sprigs thyme

3 cloves garlic, peeled and sliced

1 shallot, peeled and sliced

for the sauce

1 tbsp sunflower or olive oil

10g ($\frac{1}{2}$oz) butter

2 shallots, peeled and finely chopped

a pinch of chopped marjoram or thyme leaves

2 tsp medlar, quince or redcurrant jelly

120 ml (4fl oz) port

120 ml (4fl oz) red wine

570ml (1 pint) game or chicken stock (see p.58)

50g sun-dried cranberries (optional)

salt and pepper

for the celeriac and potato mash

1 head of 1 celeriac (450g-700g/1-1$\frac{1}{2}$lbs)

an equal weight of potatoes

50g (2oz) butter at room temperature

120ml (4fl oz) warm milk

salt, pepper and nutmeg to season

for the parsnips
2-3 large parsnips
2-3 tbsp duck fat or 1 tbsp oil and 20g (¾oz) butter
2 tbsp clear honey
salt and pepper

method

The venison component of this dish cooks really quickly so get your sauce and vegetables under way before you sear it and finish it off.

meat

Ask the butcher to remove the loins from the saddle (you can use the bones and any trimmings for making a light stock as the base for your sauce) Trim the loins well removing the membrane and marinade with a little olive oil, thyme, garlic and shallot. Because it is so tender I would not use any wine or vinegar in the marinade as it would spoil the flavour. Shake the marinade ingredients off the venison loin and brown briefly on both sides then pop it in a hot oven or under the grill for a few minutes. Season with salt and rest it for 10 minutes before carving it.

sauce

Heat the oil and butter in a pan, add the chopped shallots and cook over a low heat until soft. Add a pinch of chopped marjoram or thyme and a couple of teaspoons of medlar or quince jelly (we usually make our own but bought redcurrant jelly would have a similar effect). Add a small glass of port and a glass of red wine and reduce by half then add your game stock and reduce again to a light coating consistency (one that just coats the back of a wooden spoon). In December we add sun-dried cranberries to the sauce which give a festive look and taste. In fact the sweetness works very well with the venison.

celeriac and potato mash

Peel and cut the celeriac and potato into similar-sized pieces. If you're not using the celeriac straight away drop it into acidulated water (water with a dash of lemon juice) to stop it discolouring. Cook the celeriac and potato pieces in salted water until both are tender. Drain in a colander, cover and leave on the top of the stove to dry out before passing through a mouli. Beat in the butter and warm milk to give a smooth purée. Season well with salt, pepper and freshly grated nutmeg.

parsnips

Peel the parsnips, cut away the hard, woody core and cut into even-sized pieces. Blanch in boiling water very briefly, then fry in a little duck fat or oil and butter to colour well. They won't take long to cook. Add the honey towards the end of the cooking time and toss well together to caramelise.

to assemble

Make sure all the components are hot. Carve the venison fairly thinly, arrange on the plate with the vegetables and spoon the sauce over the meat.

Braised partridge, cabbage, bacon and lentils

Partridge is a fine bird – lighter and more delicate than pheasant and more richly flavoured than chicken. I can remember one of the best meals I ever had with the late Keith Floyd was a Sunday lunch in the restaurant he had opposite where we are now in Chandos Road where he put a big copper casserole of partridge in the middle of the table and just said 'help yourself!' (No wonder he went bust . . .)

There are two types of partridge: red-legged or grey. The greys are considered superior for eating but are harder to come by. The red-legged are slightly larger and not so expensive and therefore easier to find.

Braising partridge has the advantage that it doesn't dry out and will keep for a while if you're not ready to go to the table. A roast bird you have to eat immediately. You can choose whether or not to serve sausages with it. We make our own venison sausages which I take next door to the butcher to get made up then one of our suppliers, Steve, smokes them for me.

serves
6

ingredients

6 partridges
20g (¾oz) duck fat or oil and butter
110g (4oz) smoked bacon lardons or pancetta
2 onions, peeled and chopped
4 cloves garlic, peeled and chopped
1 leek, trimmed and sliced
2 carrots, peeled and cut into small dice
1 glass of white wine
570ml (1 pint) of chicken stock (see p.58)
1 dsp chopped thyme
2-3 tbsp chopped parsley
salt and pepper
Toulouse sausages (optional)
1 Savoy cabbage
110g (4 oz) Puy lentils
1 bay leaf

method

Brown the birds on all sides in a little duck fat or oil in a frying pan. Heat the remaining duck fat or oil and butter in a large casserole and gently cook the lardons, chopped onion, garlic, leek and carrot until soft. Season with salt and pepper. Set some aside for the lentils. Add your birds, breast side down and deglaze the frying pan with a glass of white wine and the chicken stock and add to the casserole. Add the chopped thyme, cover, and cook in a cool oven (150°C/300°F/Gas 2) for 30-40 minutes. (Grey partridges usually take longer than red-legged ones). When they are almost cooked, add the cabbage to cook and absorb the flavours as described below. You'll need to check the seasoning and add more if necessary, as the cabbage is going to absorb a fair amount of salt.

* Sometimes I also add home-made sausages to this dish but a good Toulouse sausage would be fine. I add these half way through the cooking process, allowing half a sausage per person.

cabbage

I like Savoy cabbage for this but am happy to use whatever looks good at the market. I strip off the outer leaves, cut the cabbage in half and then into wedges, leaving some of the stalk intact to hold the leaves together. I blanch them in boiling water for a few seconds, then add them to the casserole of partridge as described above.

lentils

I usually use Puy lentils which I blanch before cooking them. Tip them into your reserved, diced vegetables with a bay leaf, a sprig of thyme and some stock and season with salt and pepper. Bring up to simmering point and cook slowly until the lentils are just cooked (approximately 15 minutes).

to serve

I serve partridge whole because having braised them, the meat is very tender and you can enjoy picking the bones. Serve with the lentils and cabbage, sprinkling a little parsley over the finished dish. It should be a substantial enough main course but you could always add a few boiled potatoes – either served separately or added to the casserole at the same time as the cabbage to pick up the flavour of the sauce.

Braised pheasant with port and celery

Another Elizabeth David classic from *French Country Cooking* that I learnt to cook with Joyce Molyneux down at the Carved Angel in Dartmouth. We also cooked it at Riverside in Helford where I remember being given the comparatively 'easy' job of plucking the pheasants on my return to the kitchen after a bout of meningitis. It's a really messy job so I suggest you get a butcher or game dealer to do it for you. At Markwicks our pheasants came from a chap we used to refer to as Bill 'Game'. He was the best dresser of game I've ever known. This is a great recipe for older birds which can easily dry out.

serves
8

ingredients
1 head of 'dirty' (i.e. unwashed) celery with leaves
   (these have more flavour than the supermarket packets with the leaves cut off)
2 onions
4 cloves garlic
4 thick rashers smoked streaky bacon or 75g diced pancetta
2-3 tbsp duck fat or a mixture of olive oil and butter
4 smallish pheasants, hens or cocks
a few sprigs of thyme and a couple of bay leaves
150ml (5 fl oz) red wine
150ml (5 fl oz) inexpensive ruby port
275ml (10 fl oz) good stock (from pheasant carcasses if you have some otherwise see p.58)
150ml (5 fl oz) cream
200g (7 oz) pack of vacuum packed chestnuts (life's too short to peel chestnuts unless you have
   hundreds of willing workers...)*
about 2 tbsp finely chopped parsley
salt and pepper

you will also need a casserole or pot big enough to take 4 birds

method
Prepare the celery by washing it, peeling it with a vegetable peeler and cutting it into 1 inch (2.5cm) lengths and then into batons. (You can use the leaves by chopping them and adding them at this point, or save them for stocks or soups.) Peel and slice the onions and garlic and dice the bacon. Season the pheasants with salt and pepper.

Heat a couple of spoonfuls of duck fat or a mixture of oil and butter in the casserole and brown the pheasants all over. Remove the pheasants from the pan and set aside. Fry the bacon for a minute or two then add the onions, garlic and celery and fry gently for a further few minutes. Add the thyme, bay leaves, wine, port and stock. Season with salt and pepper.

Put the birds back in the pan breast side down and cover with a lid. Cook in a cool oven (150°C/300°F/ Gas 2) until tender – about 45 minutes to an hour (the older the birds the longer it will take).

Once the birds are cooked remove them from the pan. Skim and reduce the liquid in the pan to intensify the flavour, making sure you leave enough for the sauce and stir in the cream. Add the chestnuts and heat through. Joint the pheasants, saving the drumsticks for rissoles (see below) or the stockpot and reheat the pieces in the sauce. Sprinkle with a little chopped parsley and serve with mash and red cabbage

* A tip for removing chestnuts from a vac pack: heat the unopened pack in a pan of hot water first before you cut it open. It's difficult to take them straight from the pack when cold without them breaking up and this way they stay whole.

pheasant rissoles

In the restaurant we make rissoles from the meat from the pheasant legs and sometimes an extra whole bird. You simply pass the cooked meat through a mincer and add this to some finely chopped shallot cooked with some finely chopped mushrooms (you can chop these in a Robot-Coupe or other food processor). You can also add some of the bacon bits and vegetables from the sauce. Add some reduced pheasant stock, sauce or gravy - just enough to moisten the mixture, season it well and refrigerate it. We cut circles of pastry with a cutter and fill them with the mixture – a bit like a baby pasty – then deep fry them and serve them with a cup of consommé and a glass of dry madeira.

on hanging – or not hanging pheasants

We buy our pheasants 'long legged' or undrawn if we can and keep them in the cold room for a couple more days to enhance the flavour. No-one really hangs pheasant for long enough these days in my opinion. If they still have their innards in they keep for longer and it gives us the heart and liver to use for a paté or terrine. I wouldn't recommend buying them in feather unless you have the space to hang them, know what you're doing and have plenty of time on your hands. Plucking makes such a mess that it is best done out of doors and I don't fancy sitting in the freezing cold for hours these days! Try to buy them 'dry-plucked' if you can which keeps the skin unbroken.

Wild duck with spiced beetroot and morilles sauce

My all-time favourite game is mallard. It's a wild bird, much smaller than the average farmed duck and much richer and gamier. They're now quite hard to get hold of because of an EEC ruling that they can't be shot with lead shot so suppliers have to use much more expensive ammunition which increases the price. We find people are quite happy to sell the birds so long as it covers the cost of the shot! I like to roast the breasts and serve them rare but I take the legs off beforehand and braise them otherwise they can be tough. Allow half a bird per person.

serves	6

ingredients	3 mallard
	2 tbsp sunflower oil or duck fat
	110g (4oz) finely chopped onion, carrot, leek and celery (a *mirepoix*)*
	a sprig of thyme
	275ml (½ pint) game or chicken stock
	for the sauce
	25g (1oz) dried morilles mushrooms soaked in 275ml warm stock (see p.58)
	2 shallots, peeled and finely chopped
	50ml (2fl oz) dry madeira (or sherry will do)
	75ml (3fl oz) double cream
	for the beetroot
	5-6 good sized beetroot
	olive oil
	2 sprigs of thyme
	1-2 dsp grated horseradish (from a jar is fine)
	a few drops of balsamic vinegar
	1 tbsp crème fraîche
	salt and pepper

method

Take the legs off the duck, leaving just the crown (the two breasts on the remaining carcass.) You can cut away the backbone and wishbone – easiest with scissors or get your butcher to do it – so that the breasts sit upright in the tin and are easier to carve once roasted. (You can use the carcasses later for making stocks).

duck legs

You need to braise the legs before cooking the breasts. Season them, brown them in a frying pan in a little oil then transfer them to a small casserole. Fry a little *mirepoix** of carrot, onion, leeks and celery in the remaining fat and add to the legs. Deglaze the pan with some stock, pour over the legs, bring up to simmering point then turn the heat right down and cook on top of the stove or in a slow oven (150°C/300°F/Gas 2) for approximately 45 minutes. (The stock you have here will be useful for making your sauce but keep a little back for re-heating the legs when you're serving up).

* a *mirepoix* is a finely diced selection of vegetables that chefs tend to have to hand. If you chop up an onion, carrot, leek and a stick of celery you'll end up with more than you need but can always use the rest in a soup or a stew.

sauce

Having pre-soaked the morilles mushrooms in a little warm stock I usually cut them in half before cooking them gently in butter with some finely chopped shallot. Add the madeira or sherry and the strained liquid from soaking the morilles and some of the cooking liquor from the legs. Simmer the sauce until reduced to a light coating consistency that will cover the back of a spoon, add the cream and warm through.

beetroot

I roast the washed beetroots in the oven whole and unpeeled. Put them in a roasting tray with some seasoning, thyme and olive oil, cover with foil and bake at 200°C/400°F/Gas 6 for about 45 minutes. Once they're cooked, leave them to cool, peel them and cut into dice. When I serve the dish I warm the diced beetroot up with grated horseradish and a little balsamic vinegar to sharpen them and stir in a tablespoon of crème fraîche.

duck breasts

Brush the crowns with a little melted butter and place, breast side downwards in a roasting tin on top of the stove then transfer them breast side up to a hot oven (200°C/400°F/Gas 6). These really do not take very long to cook at all (approximately 5-10 mins): they need to be served rare otherwise they toughen up. Salt, cover with foil and leave in a warm place for 10 minutes before removing the breasts from the bone and carving them as thinly as possible.

to serve

Heat through the beetroot, braised legs and the sauce. I usually put the beetroot on the plate first with the leg on top and then the sauce and arrange the duck slices alongside. Make sure each portion has a few morilles. This is lovely with a layered potato cake or sauté potatoes and a green leafy vegetable like cavolo nero.

tip

I don't put any seasoning into my sauces at all – the flavour comes from reduction (cooking until the volume of liquid is reduced). You need to take care that you don't over-reduce them though or they can become over-intense. If the flavour is too strong add a bit of extra stock or cream or, if you have neither, a splash of corporation stock (tap water) will do the job!

Sweets

Cheese: Stilton with biscuits	80
Home-made blackberry ice-cream	90
St. Emilion au chocolat	90
Crème Caramel	80
Fresh pineapple with Kirsch	85
Home-made mince tart	85
Candied oranges	85

Coffee: 30p. per cup.

1980 Autumn desserts from Bistro Twenty One

" To say he's not really into desserts is an understatement. He's a legend but when it comes to desserts he's a very traditional man. He'll remember a time when I wanted to put chickpea ice cream on the menu and he said 'not a chance!' "

Charlotte Marrifield - former pastry chef.

Pears in red wine with rice pudding

I've always liked pears but we only use them in the autumn - they don't taste as good at any other time of year. Partnering them with rice pudding makes them real comfort food. Any leftover pears in wine can be turned into jellies.

serves   8

ingredients
1 bottle of red wine
350-400g (12-14oz) granulated sugar
8 ripe eating pears such as Williams or Comice (it's important these aren't unripe)
1 vanilla pod, split
1 cinnamon stick
4-5 cloves

method
Pour the wine into a large saucepan, tip in the sugar and place over a low heat for the sugar to dissolve. Add the cloves, cinnamon stick and vanilla pod, split lengthways. Bring up to simmering point. While you're dissolving the sugar and infusing the spices, peel the pears being careful to leave the stalk intact.

Add the pears to the red wine and cover with greaseproof paper using a plate to keep them submerged. Bring the wine back up to a very low simmer until the pears are cooked (approximately 10-15 minutes). When the pears are soft leave them to cool in the wine to intensify the colour.

Remove the pears carefully and transfer to a serving dish. Reduce the wine by approximately a third. Pour the wine over the pears and serve hot with warm rice pudding (see opposite) or cold with ice-cream, crème fraîche or cream.

Rice pudding

This method produces a creamy rice pudding without a skin but you can always cook it in a cool oven if you prefer one. I can remember as children we always used to fight over it.

serves   8

ingredients   100g (3½oz) butter
150g (5oz) pudding rice
1.5 litres (2½ pints) whole milk (i.e. not semi-skimmed)
225ml (8fl oz) double cream
½ a vanilla pod
pinch of salt
125g (4½oz) granulated sugar

method   Wash the rice. Melt the butter in a large heavy-bottomed pan. Put the rice into the pan with the vanilla pod and pinch of salt and stir to coat the rice with the butter.

Add the milk and cream and bring up to simmering point. I then cover the surface with a butter paper and leave on a very low heat for approximately two hours, stirring from time to time to stop it catching and check how it is progressing. The butter paper stops a skin forming but you could also cook it in a cool oven (150°C/300°F/Gas 2) if you find this easier.

Once it is thick and creamy stir in the sugar to dissolve it.

We had a girl who washed up for us for a couple of years who was most upset if she didn't get the rice pudding pan with a hefty amount of rice pudding left in it to finish off!

Warm Tunisian orange cake

This recipe came from one of our pastry chefs Katie Barton, who found it in an article by Sophie Grigson. It has pretty much remained a permanent fixture. It's incredibly easy – you just mix all the ingredients together and bake them – in fact the most difficult part is getting the candied peel right and you don't need to do that if you don't want to. We have customers who come in for lunch every time they see it on the menu. One bought a whole cake for her boss after he said he'd enjoyed it!

serves   8

ingredients   40g (1½oz) dried breadcrumbs (see opposite)
                200g (7oz) caster sugar
                100g (3½oz) ground almonds
                1 level tsp baking powder
                200ml (7fl oz) sunflower oil
                4 medium eggs
                zest of one orange (preferably unwaxed)
                zest of half a lemon (again, unwaxed for preference)
                for the syrup
                2 tbsp lemon juice
                4 tbsp orange juice
                50g (2oz) sugar
                ½ cinnamon stick
                5-6 cloves
                2 star anise

                you will also need a lightly greased 21cm (8½in) spring release cake tin lined with non-stick baking parchment.

method   Put all the dry ingredients in the bowl of an electric mixer (or an ordinary mixing bowl if you have a hand-held mixer). In another bowl beat the eggs lightly then beat in the oil. Add the liquid to the dry ingredients and beat well then pour into the prepared tin and place in a COLD oven (sounds weird but this is right!) Turn the oven to 180°C/350°F/Gas 4 and bake for about 1-1¼ hours until well risen and browned. Meanwhile put the ingredients for the syrup into a pan, slowly bring to the boil and cook for a couple of minutes without stirring.

                When the cake is cooked take it out of the oven and pour over the syrup while it is still hot, leaving the spices on the cake to decorate. Leave to cool a little before removing from the tin.

to serve   We serve this with candied orange peel, orange slices and mascarpone cream (opposite) but you could simply serve it with whipped cream sweetened with a little orange liqueur if you like. You can eat it warm or cold.

candied orange zest	Finely pare the rind off a couple of oranges. Blanch the pieces twice in boiling water then cut them into strips and cook in stock syrup (below) until they are tender but not too soft.
orange slices	Take two oranges and cut off the very top and bottom with a sharp knife. Cut round the orange removing the peel and pith then cut in between the segments so the oranges pieces come out cleanly without any pith.
orange mascarpone cream	Tip the mascarpone into a bowl – about 1 tablespoon per person – and add just enough orange liqueur (Cointreau, Grand Marnier – whatever you've got) to give you a spoonable consistency. Add a little grated orange rind and check for sweetness adding a few drops more liqueur or sugar syrup to taste
stock syrup	Put equal amounts of water and sugar into a saucepan and place over a low heat, stirring occasionally, until all the grains of sugar have dissolved. Bring to the boil and boil for 3 minutes without stirring then take off the heat and cool. (If you stir it at this stage the syrup will crystallise and go cloudy). Pour into a clean jar or plastic container and refrigerate.
dried breadcrumbs	You can buy dried breadcrumbs but we make our own by putting leftover bread on a tray over the stove to dry out (you could do this in a low oven), then in a food mixer and sieve. As well as this recipe we use them for egging and crumbing, coating fishcakes etc.

Walnut and treacle tart

This is a Jane Grigson recipe (from *Good Things*) and my favourite treacle tart. I haven't done anything to it - it's too good to change: just a nice rich satisfying dessert - a real man's pudding. You can make both the pastry and the filling in a food processor though in George's day we weren't allowed to. It all had to be done by hand.

serves

6-8

ingredients

225g (8oz) walnut halves or broken walnuts
the zest and juice of a lemon (about 3tbsp)
a pinch of salt
110g (4oz) butter at room temperature
110g (4oz) soft dark muscovado sugar
175g (6oz) golden syrup*
3 medium eggs, lightly beaten
clotted cream or vanilla ice cream to serve
a 20cm (8in) pre-baked sweet pastry case (see p.61)

method

Blitz the walnuts in a food processor – not too finely – then turn into a bowl and add the lemon zest and juice and a pinch of salt. Cream the butter and sugar, again in the processor and then gradually add eggs, being careful not to curdle the mixture. (If it begins to curdle add a bit of the walnut mix.) Finally add the walnuts and golden syrup and mix carefully.

Turn into the pre-baked pastry case and cook in a low oven (150°C/300°F/Gas 2) for about 1 ½ - 2 hours until just firm. If the top hasn't browned turn the oven up a bit. Serve with clotted cream or vanilla ice cream.

* The easiest way to measure golden syrup is to warm the tin by standing it in a pan of hot water and heating it gently on the stove then place a small pan on the scales and spoon the syrup into the pan. It's much easier to control while it's warm. Keep the pan in a warm place on the side of the stove while making the tart.

St Emilion au chocolat

Another recipe from my George Perry-Smith days – a rich chocolate mousse with a good whack of brandy. It's lighter than the famous Elizabeth David version.

I seem to remember he adapted the recipe from the back of an England Glory matchbox and added the macaroons which is the other thing Saint-Emilion is famous for (apart from the wine). We've been doing it for so long it's referred to as 'Saints' in the restaurant – in fact Judy occasionally gets to the stage of saying 'You're not doing Saints *again*!'.

Although it's a really simple recipe you have to be careful not to overheat the chocolate – when I make it in the restaurant I don't do any other jobs at the same time.

serves

8 portions

ingredients

225g 70% dark chocolate
  (I used to use Chocolate Menier but you could use a bar like Lindt's Excellence)
2 tbsp strong coffee such as double espresso
3 largeish (6-8cm) shop-bought macaroons
  (the old fashioned kind with squidgy centres not amaretti)
25ml brandy (cooking brandy is fine: I wouldn't put Hine '62 into it!)
4 medium eggs
whipped cream to serve

method

You can either make this in individual coffee cups or small ramekins or in a single deep bowl.

Break the chocolate into pieces and put in a pan with 110ml warm water and the coffee and melt on the edge of the stove (or place in a bowl over hot water making sure the base of the bowl doesn't touch the water). Temperature is critical to this recipe: blood heat is what you want.

Meanwhile break up the macaroons and sprinkle with the brandy. Separate the eggs and whisk the whites to a peak.

Mix the yolks into the warm chocolate then carefully fold in the whites. This needs to be done quickly, while the chocolate is at the right temperature. Layer the chocolate mixture with the broken macaroons, finishing with a piece of macaroon on top. (If I bake my own macaroons I make some small ones for this purpose.) Top with a spoonful of whipped cream.

Stocks

Some useful basics which are used in a number of our dishes. They're second-nature, I appreciate, to a restaurant kitchen – and can be daunting to attempt at home but they do make a difference . .

Meat stock

Good stocks are at the heart of all professional kitchens. They give you a much better, rounder flavour than a cube. It is not essential to use beef bones for a beef dish or lamb bones for a lamb dish but it is nice to do so if you have them. Chicken stock is the lightest of all meat stocks and therefore the most versatile and can be used in other meat dishes. Whereas I would never use beef or lamb stock in a chicken dish I would use chicken stock in other meat dishes. You should be able to get bones from a good butcher.

ingredients

1-2 kg (2lb 4oz - 4lb 8oz) of raw chicken, beef, veal or lamb bones,
2 onions, 2 carrots, 4 cloves of garlic, 2 sticks of celery and some leek ends and coarse outer leaves

method

Roast the bones in a hot (200°C/400°F/Gas 6) oven for about 25 minutes until well browned, turning them half way through. Transfer to a large pan. Chop up the vegetables, add to the original roasting tin and roast until lightly coloured (about 15 minutes). Add to the pan. Deglaze the roasting tin with water, tip over the bones and vegetables, top up with cold water, bring to the boil and skim off any froth. Add a few peppercorns, some thyme stalks and a couple of bayleaves. Bring to the boil and leave uncovered on a very low heat, for 3-4 hours, skimming from time to time (or, alternatively, covered in the simmering oven of an AGA overnight). Strain the stock and skim thoroughly to remove the fat. Reduce until you get the intensity of flavour you want. You can also freeze this stock.

* For an extra-intense stock instead of water you can use a batch of previously made stock to cook your roast bones and vegetables – something I tend to do with pheasant stock or if I'm making a consommé.

Fish stock

Homemade fish stock is what makes our fish soup taste as good as it does but I'm not pretending it's not a chore. It's worth making this amount so you have some extra to freeze. The key thing is to get the right kind of bones – you don't want bones from oily fish like mackerel and even plaice will make a stock taste bitter. I also don't use shellfish trimmings as so many people can't eat shellfish. The best fish bones to use are from prime white fish like turbot, halibut, brill, sole and John Dory – the better the fish, the better the stock.

ingredients

1kg (2lb 4oz) fish heads, bones and trimmings (see above), 1 onion, 1 leek (trimmed and washed), a stick of celery, any fennel trimmings, parsley stalks, 2tbsp olive oil and a good knob of butter, a few black peppercorns and a couple of bayleaves

method

Remove the gills from any fish heads (insert your fingers behind the gill, twist and pull or simply cut out with scissors). Wash the bones several times to get rid of the blood (otherwise it will make the stock cloudy). Cut up the vegetables roughly. Pour the oil in a large pan, add the butter and cook the vegetables and bones over a low heat until the bones start to go opaque. Add the peppercorns and bayleaves, cover with cold water - and a little white wine if you have some (although I don't tend to bother as I usually use white wine in the sauces that use this stock). Bring to the boil, skim then turn down the heat to the lowest setting you can for just 15-20 minutes then strain.

* Don't be tempted to cook the stock longer. It over-extracts the flavour from the bones and makes them bitter. Cool and refrigerate or freeze for up to 2 months.

Sweet and savoury pastry

Stephen at Bistro Twenty One in the early 1980's

I find the easiest way to stop the pastry shrinking when you bake it is to leave it untrimmed then trim it after you've baked the filled tart, the idea being to get as much filling in as possible.

We usually have at least one tart on the menu – sometimes a sweet and a savoury one. I generally make the pastry in a Robot-Coupe though I mix in the liquid by hand. I find the easiest way to stop the pastry shrinking when you bake it is to leave it untrimmed then trim it after you've baked the filled tart, the idea being to get as much filling in as possible. I also line the case with a double layer of cling film before putting in the baking beans (which makes it easier to lift the beans out). Like Fiona I didn't believe it would work but it simply crinkles up and keeps the pastry firmly in place.

Sweet shortcrust pastry

Enough to line a 20cm (8 in) flan tin or ring

ingredients   225g (8oz) plain flour, 2tbsp icing sugar, 110g (4oz) chilled unsalted butter, cut into small cubes, 1 medium egg, beaten

method   Sieve the flour and icing sugar in the bowl of a food processor, add the butter and pulse until breadcrumb consistency. Add the egg and pulse again. If the mixture isn't coming together add a tablespoon of water. Rest for at least half an hour in the fridge before using. Roll out and line a 20cm (8 in) flan tin or ring leaving the pastry overhanging the edges and chill for 30 minutes in the freezer. Line the pastry case with a double layer of cling film, scatter with baking beans and bake for 15 minutes at 200°C/400°F/Gas 6 then remove the cling film and beans and return the tart to the oven to crisp up until it is lightly browned. Fill as described in the recipe then trim off the overhanging pastry after the tart is cooked.

Shortcrust pastry

ingredients   225g (8oz) plain flour, 150g (5oz) butter, chilled and cut into small cubes, a pinch of salt

method   Put the flour, salt and butter into the bowl of a food processor and pulse until breadcrumb consistency. Turn into a mixing bowl and add just enough water to bring the mixture together (between 4 and 6 tablespoons depending on the time of year. You tend to need less water in the summer). Don't overwork the mixture - handle it as lightly as possible - then follow the method above for rolling out, chilling and baking the pastry.

Wine stories

Stephen's robust style of cooking has always been much admired by wine lovers, not least the late, great Bill Baker who supplied us with wine from our early days. He often used to turn up with half a dozen wines for us to try and would always tell us which would suit our food best or if a new vintage wasn't as good as the last one and we should take it off the list. He even used to comment on the food. If Stephen wanted some feedback on a new dish he'd always give him an honest critique.

Occasionally he'd ring up to say he was bringing some special wines and tell Stephen what he wanted to eat with them. Also Stephen went and cooked for him in his home – he catered for his wedding and his 40th and 50th birthday bashes which he held jointly with Simon Hopkinson. Many other well-known chefs lent a hand too.

When we first started in the '80s people didn't drink wine like they do now and weren't nearly as knowledgeable. I remember we used to buy litre bottles for our house wine from a chap who used to go to France and pick it up, but it was pretty good. We've always taken the view that our house wine should be something we would happily drink ourselves. In fact we taste everything on the list.

We still buy from Reid and from another local Bristol firm Vine Trail which sells some very good wines. The owners, Nick and Cath Brookes, buy from relatively unknown growers and we like the idea of supporting a very small independent business like us. We try to steer clear of the very well-known names that are stocked by the supermarkets.

We keep the list short and the prices reasonable. I know our mark-up is less than a lot of other restaurants. We always have a number of half bottles too so that a table of two can have the option of ordering a red and a white. I know a lot of customers appreciate that (as we do ourselves as Stephen generally orders meat as a main course whereas I'd rather have fish). We have to make quite an effort to find good half bottles - not so many are produced these days as they are less cost-effective for the producers.

Although the list is mainly French we have stocked more new world wine over the years. I particularly like Cullen's Semillon-Sauvignon from the Margaret River in Western Australia. Stephen prefers reds especially big Rhone wines like Hermitage. When we were at Bistro Twenty One we did buy a few cases of wine to lay down but it terrified me. When Stephen spent £95 on a case of Hermitage la Chapelle 1978 it seemed a fortune. I was furious with him!

Over the years we've been on a number of epic wine trips although sadly we've never managed to get to Krug, even though we've been invited. I can recall one where Stephen flew to Reims for lunch then down to Cognac for a couple of days on an executive jet. I remember him phoning me from some giant marble bathroom. When he arrived back I could smell the alcoholic fumes before I could see him!

When we go on holiday we always go and visit local winemakers. It's something we really enjoy, especially if they are one of our suppliers. It was a great pleasure, for instance, to sit in a square in Jurançon in south-west France not so long ago, drinking a glass of Jurançon that we have on our list. Good wine is a great treat!

Judy Markwick

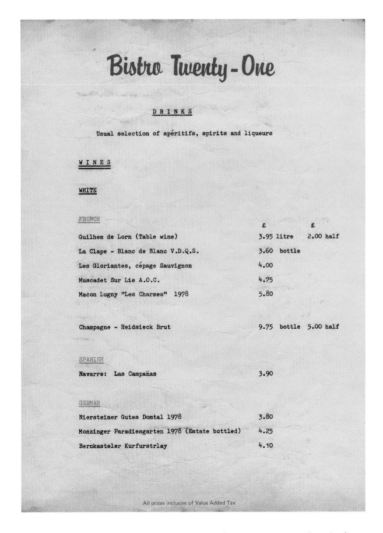

Bistro Twenty One Wine List, 1980

Acknowledgements

My thanks to the many people who have been involved in the production of this book, particularly to Fiona Beckett, whose idea it was in the first place and without whom it would never have been written. In spite of my vagueness about how to write recipes, she has been able to interpret and coax out of me what has been in my head! Thanks too to Vanessa Courtier, the designer, and printers Cromwell Press. Testers and tasters: our daughters Claire and partner Leighton and Zoë and her husband Ben; regular customers Jennifer and Colin and Jenny in our kitchen. Claire has also kindly helped with the unenviable task of proof-reading. We are also very grateful to Simon Hopkinson for writing such a generous foreword and those who have allowed us to use their recipes: Heather Perry-Smith on behalf of George Perry-Smith estate, Joyce Molyneux who taught me at The Carved Angel, Jill Norman on behalf of the Elizabeth David estate and Sophie Grigson for use of her own recipe and that of her mother, Jane Grigson. If there's anyone we have inadvertently overlooked or incorrectly attributed may we apologise?

Our suppliers

We have had a longstanding relationship with most of our suppliers, many of whom started their businesses 30 years ago, around the same time as we did. Chief of these is Steve Downey of Chef Direct at Barrow Gurney who supplies us with fish, meat and some of our game - though we have other suppliers such as Roger Davis (known to us as Roger Rabbit) a game dealer *extraordinaire* who brings in rabbits and venison that's to die for.

Steve is someone who just never stands still. He is constantly coming up with new ideas and dreaming up trouble for himself but he's passionate about his produce, and knows I will treat it well and simply. He's always come to our restaurants when he's wanted to impress people. I remember him bringing Albert Roux to Markwicks for lunch and another time being filmed with me, delivering a Glenarm salmon which he used to bring in the early days in an old GPO van! He also gets THE BEST diver-caught plaice from a sub aqua diving club which dives off the Dorset coast. They're all getting on in age now so I'm not sure how we're going to get our plaice once they can no longer get into their rubber suits!

Most of our fruit and vegetables have been supplied by Mrs Bennett of Pawsons in Gloucester Road. Thirty years ago her daughter Sue was just a schoolgirl and only used to work on Saturday mornings and is now running the shop.

We also buy from the Wednesday Bristol Farmers' market at Corn Street. Our herbs and the best salad leaves I have ever seen come from Anthony Lyman-Dixon of Arne Herbs and more salad leaves, vegetables and some fruit from Leigh Court Farm.

For cheese we've always relied on Anne Marie of the Fine Cheese Company in Bath who sources cheese from local producers such as Mary Holbrook of Sleight Farm, Keen's Cheddar, Sharpham and Robin Congdon of Ticklemore Cheese. (We've always stuck to British cheeses at Culinaria, trying to showcase cheese from the West Country. This is true of all our produce wherever possible.)

Finally several customers bring us in their own produce from their allotments and gardens, such as figs, crab apples, medlars, sloes and quince in return for a jar or two of preserves, for which we're always very grateful.

Our warm thanks to you all.